Florida

Civics

End-of-Course Assessment
Test Preparation Workbook

Grade 7

HOLT McDOUGAL

HOUGHTON MIFFLIN HARCOURT

Text Acknowledgments

Excerpt from "How To Spend It" by Will Rogers from *The Tulsa World*. Text copyright © 1925. Reprinted by permission of Will Rogers Memorial Museum.

Table of Contents

To the Student

As a student in Florida, you will take the Florida End-of-Course Assessment for Civics at the end of this school year. To help you get ready for the test, Holt McDougal Social Studies has created the *Florida Civics End-of-Course Assessment Test Prep Workbook*. Included in this book are test-taking strategies and practice tests. Completing these materials as assigned will help you to succeed on exam day.

Before doing any of the practice tests, take some time to go over the test-taking strategies found at the front of the book. These pages will introduce you to the format of the Florida End-of-Course Assessment for Civics. They will also teach you how to approach the different kinds of questions on the test. Completing the practice questions on these pages will help you get the most from what you learn.

This book also contains four practice tests. Each practice test consists of 48 multiple-choice questions that cover the Florida Next Generation Sunshine State Standards for Civics and Government. These questions cover what you have already learned in class and will help you remember the information you will be expected to know for the test.

Finally, at the end of this workbook, you will find seven unit activities, one for each unit of Holt McDougal's *Florida Civics in Practice*. Each unit activity includes five multiple choice questions and one document-based question developed to reinforce your mastery of the Florida Next Generation Sunshine State Standards for Civics and Government.

The Florida End-of-Course Assessment for Civics

The purpose of the Florida End-of-Course Assessment for Civics is to test your knowledge about government and the rights and responsibilities of citizens at the local, state, and national levels. The test will consist of 48 multiple-choice questions. Each question supports one of the Florida Next Generation Sunshine State Standards for Civics and Government.

Each question on the Florida End-of-Course Assessment will also address Low, Moderate, and High levels of "Depth of Knowledge." These levels do not refer to a level of difficulty. Rather, they refer to the thinking and reasoning skills you will need to use to answer the question. The chart below summarizes some of the thinking skills related to each level. Becoming familiar with these levels will help you think about which skills you will need to use to solve each multiple-choice question.

DEPTH OF KNOWLEDGE

Level	Thinking Skills
Low	• Identify or recall a fact, a definition, or a simple procedure • Use a chart, table, diagram, graph, or image to recall or recognize information • Identify the characteristics of a group, place, or event
Moderate	• Analyze cause-and-effect relationships • Identify the significance of events, actions, personalities, and ideas • Categorize people, places, events, and ideas • Determine the relationships between events, actions, personalities, and ideas • Explain problems, patterns, and issues
High	• Solve problems • Generalize • Draw conclusions • Provide justifications for events and actions • Make predictions • Analyze the effects of ideas and events • Recognize and explain misconceptions • Analyze similarities and differences

Test-Taking Strategies and Practice

You can improve your test-taking skills by practicing the strategies discussed in this section. First, read the tips in the left-hand column. Then apply them to the practice items in the right-hand column.

Multiple Choice

Florida's End-of-Course Assessment for Civics contains 48 multiple-choice items. Each multiple-choice item will consist of a single stem that asks a question relating to civics. Four possible answer choices will appear below the stem. Only one of these choices is the correct answer. The other choices, called *distracters*, are incorrect.

❶ Read the stem carefully. Determine what the question is asking.

❷ Look for key words and facts in the stem. They will help you determine the correct answer.

❸ Read each answer choice. Eliminate answer choices that you know are incorrect.

❹ Some stems will include a prompt that will help you answer the question. Read the stem. Then read or study the prompt carefully to select the correct answer choice.

❺ Watch for words such as *all*, *always*, and *never*. Answers choices that include these words usually are incorrect. These words indicate that the correct answer must be an undisputed fact. In social studies, few facts are undisputed.

answers: 1 (B); 2 (D); 3 (B)

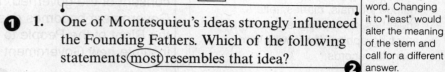

stem

Most is a key word. Changing it to "least" would alter the meaning of the stem and call for a different answer.

❶ **1.** One of Montesquieu's ideas strongly influenced the Founding Fathers. Which of the following statements (most) resembles that idea? **❷**

❸ | answer choices |

- **A.** People and rulers are partners in a social contract.
- **B.** There should be separation of powers within a government.
- **C.** Natural laws are more important than a government's laws.
- **D.** The ideas of Enlightenment thinkers should be the basis for American education.

2. Use the information in the box to answer the question.

 | prompt |

Speaker 1 "Everyone is entitled to equal justice under the law."
Speaker 2 "The United States is a government of laws not one person."
Speaker 3 "A person's fate should not rest in the hands of a king."
Speaker 4 "No person is above the law."

Which constitutional principle is being discussed?

- **A.** individual rights
- **B.** minority rule
- **C.** due process
- **D.** rule of law

3. How is a public-interest group different from a special-interest group?

Absolute words, such as *always*, often signal an incorrect choice.

- **A.** Public-interest groups are (always) funded **❺** with public or government money.
- **B.** Public-interest groups promote the interest of the general public rather than a small part of the public.
- **C.** Public-interest groups provide more information to the public than special-interest groups do.
- **D.** Public-interest groups represent the interests of a particular group of citizens.

x

x

x

Primary Sources

Primary sources are materials that have been written or made by people who were at historical events, either as observers or participants. Primary sources include journals, diaries, letters, speeches, newspaper articles, autobiographies, laws, wills, and financial records.

❶ For quotations and excerpts from texts, be sure to read the source line first. Information about the author and source will help you understand the quotation.

❷ Skim the quotation or excerpt to get an idea of what it is about. (This is an excerpt from the Declaration of Independence.)

❸ Next, skim the stem and answer choices. This will help you focus your reading and more easily locate answers.

❹ Then, read the entire quotation or excerpt carefully. Use active reading strategies. For instance, ask and answer questions on the content as you read.

❺ Reread the selection if any of it is unclear to you. Use context clues to help you understand unfamiliar words.

❻ Finally, apply the strategies you learned for answering multiple-choice questions.

---

❷ ❹

"We hold these truths to be self-evident, that all men are created equal, that they are endowed by their Creator with certain unalienable Rights, that among these are Life, Liberty, and the pursuit of Happiness. That to secure these rights, Governments are instituted among Men, deriving their just powers from the consent of the governed, That whenever any Form of Government becomes destructive of these ends, it is the Right of the People to alter or to abolish it, and to institute new Government . . ."

❶ —from the Declaration of Independence

❺ From the context, you conclude that "unalienable" means "natural".

1. Which phrase reveals the Founding Fathers' beliefs about the source of government power?

❸
❻

A. "We hold these truths to be self-evident"

B. "endowed by their Creator with certain unalienable Rights"

C. "to secure these rights, Governments are instituted among Men"

D. "deriving their powers from the consent of the governed"

2. Which idea is *best* expressed in this excerpt?

A. Montesquieu's theory of separation of power

B. John Locke's theory of natural rights

C. the idea of liberty expressed in the English Bill of Rights

D. the idea of limited government expressed in Magna Carta

answers: 1 (D); 2 (B)

Charts

Charts present information in visual form. There are several types of charts, including tables, flow charts, Venn diagrams, and infographics. The chart most commonly found on exams is the table. Tables organize information in columns and rows for easy viewing.

1 Read the title and identify the broad subject of the chart.

2 Read the column and row headings and any other labels. These will provide more details about the subject of the chart.

3 Note how the information in the chart is organized.

4 Compare and contrast the information from column to column and row to row.

5 Try to draw conclusions from the information in the chart.

6 Read the questions carefully and then study the chart again to determine the answers.

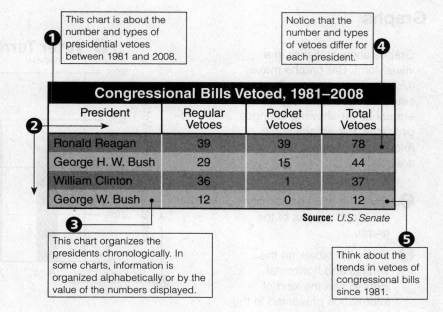

1 This chart is about the number and types of presidential vetoes between 1981 and 2008.

4 Notice that the number and types of vetoes differ for each president.

Congressional Bills Vetoed, 1981–2008			
President	Regular Vetoes	Pocket Vetoes	Total Vetoes
Ronald Reagan	39	39	78
George H. W. Bush	29	15	44
William Clinton	36	1	37
George W. Bush	12	0	12

Source: *U.S. Senate*

3 This chart organizes the presidents chronologically. In some charts, information is organized alphabetically or by the value of the numbers displayed.

5 Think about the trends in vetoes of congressional bills since 1981.

6

1. According to the chart, who had the most vetoes during his presidential term?

   A. Ronald Reagan
   B. George H. W. Bush
   C. William Clinton
   D. George W. Bush

2. Which of the following best describes the trend in the number of total vetoes by each president since 1981?

   A. increased
   B. decreased
   C. dropped to zero
   D. stayed the same

answers: 1 (A); 2 (B)

Graphs

Graphs show statistics in a visual form. Bar graphs make it easy to compare numbers or sets of numbers. Line graphs are useful for showing changes over time. Pie graphs show relationships among the parts of a whole.

❶ Read the title and identify the broad subject of the graph.

❷ Study the labels on the vertical and horizontal axes to see the kind of information presented in the graph. Note the intervals between amounts and between dates. This will help you read the graph more efficiently.

❸ Look at the source line and evaluate the reliability of the information in the graph.

❹ Draw conclusions and make inferences based on information in the graph.

❺ Read the questions carefully and then study the graph again to determine the answers.

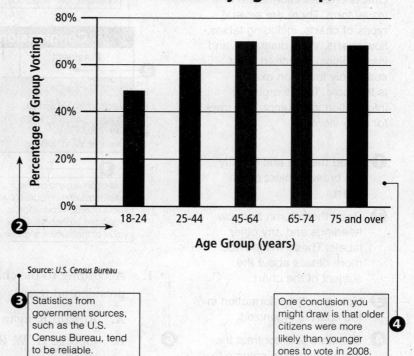

❶ Voter Turnout by Age Group, 2008

Source: *U.S. Census Bureau*

❸ Statistics from government sources, such as the U.S. Census Bureau, tend to be reliable.

❹ One conclusion you might draw is that older citizens were more likely than younger ones to vote in 2008.

1. According to the graph, which age group had the highest voter turnout?

    A. 18 to 24 years

    B. 25 to 44 years

    C. 45 to 64 years

    D. 65 to 74 years

2. What percentage of Americans aged 25 to 44 voted in 2008?

    A. 48.5 percent

    B. 60.0 percent

    C. 69.2 percent

    D. 72.4 percent

answers: 1 (D); 2 (B)

Maps

There are many different kinds of maps. Three of the most common are physical maps, political maps, and thematic maps. Physical maps are used to display physical features, such as mountains, rivers, lakes, seas, and oceans. Political maps show countries and the political divisions within them—states or provinces, for example. They also show the location of major cities. Thematic, or special-purpose, maps focus on a particular topic, such as population density, election results, or major battles in a war. The thematic map on this page shows the results of the 2008 presidential election in Florida.

① Read the title of the map to identify the area shown and the subject covered.

② Examine the labels on the map to find more information on the map's subject.

③ Study the legend to find the meaning of any symbols, colors, or shading used on the map.

④ Look at the map and try to identify patterns. If included, use the compass rose to determine directions and the scale to determine distance between places shown on the map.

⑤ Read the questions carefully and then study the map again to determine the answers.

② The labels identify major cities in Florida.

① 2008 Election Results in Florida Counties

Tallahassee ★   Jacksonville

Tampa

Miami

③ This legend indicates the shadings that represent each candidate on the map, as well as the candidates' party affiliations and election results.

Candidate	Political Affiliation	Counties Won	Popular Votes
Barack Obama	Democratic	15	4,282,074
John McCain	Republican	52	4,045,624
TOTAL		67	8,327,698

—— County boundaries

④ Notice that Barack Obama, who claimed Florida's 27 electoral votes, won more popular votes but fewer counties than John McCain.

⑤ 1. According to the map, Barack Obama won a block of four counties surrounding which city?

    A. Jacksonville

    B. Miami

    C. Tallahassee

    D. Tampa

2. What percentage of the popular vote did John McCain win?

    A. 22 percent

    B. 49 percent

    C. 51 percent

    D. 78 percent

answers: 1 (B); 2 (B)

Test 1

1. Why did the Founding Fathers separate the power to make, enforce, and interpret laws between different branches of government?

   A. to prevent one branch of government from becoming too powerful

   B. to make the national government more efficient

   C. to increase the power of the presidency

   D. to ensure that Congress would act according to the will of the people

2. What pamphlet denounced British rule and fanned the flames of revolution?

   A. Magna Carta

   B. *Two Treatises of Government*

   C. Mayflower Compact

   D. *Common Sense*

3. Use the quotation to answer the question.

   > "THE HORRID MASSACRE IN BOSTON, Perpetrated in the evening of the fifth day of March, 1770, by soldiers of the Twenty-ninth Regiment, which with the Fourteenth Regiment were then quartered there; with some observations on the state of things prior to that catastrophe."
   >
   > —anonymous account, *A Short Narrative of the Horrid Massacre in Boston*, 1770

   Who **most likely** wrote this passage and for what reason?

   A. a Redcoat, to describe the risks faced by soldiers

   B. a Patriot, to raise fears about the British army in the colonies

   C. a Loyalist, to gain support for quartering British troops

   D. an eyewitness, to promote nonviolent protest

4. Consider this situation: On January 25, 2011, widespread pro-democracy demonstrations began in Egypt. For 18 days, hundreds of thousands of Egyptians took to the streets, demanding free elections, free speech, and an end to government corruption, police brutality, and President Hosni Mubarak's regime. Finally, on February 11, Mubarak resigned. Which of the following ideas expressed in the U.S. Declaration of Independence **best supports** the actions of the Egyptian people?

   A. The government grants rights to life, liberty, and the pursuit of happiness.

   B. Citizens have a right to overthrow a government that violates their natural rights.

   C. All citizens are created equal and have unalienable rights.

   D. Citizens must consent to follow the rules of a social contract.

5. What is the **most likely** reason it was difficult to pass laws under the Articles of Confederation?

   A. Passage required a unanimous vote of the 13 states.

   B. Passage required the votes of 9 of the 13 states.

   C. The government did not have a legislature.

   D. Americans were content to follow British laws.

6. The Preamble of the Constitution lists six goals, including which of the following?

   A. to separate from Britain

   B. to form a more perfect union

   C. to decide who can be a Supreme Court justice

   D. to decrease the power of the federal government

7. Use the table to answer the question.

   Title:_____?_____

Branch	Power
Legislative	Makes laws
Executive	Carries out laws
Judicial	Interprets laws

   Which of the following best completes the title of this table?

   A. The Federal System

   B. Separation of Powers

   C. Checks and Balances

   D. Popular Sovereignty

8. Use the information in the box to answer the question.

   > **Speaker 1:** "We can't ratify the Constitution. It has no bill of rights!"
   >
   > **Speaker 2:** "I think the states should have more power."
   >
   > **Speaker 3:** "We just fought for liberty. Why submit to a new tyrant?"

   Who are the speakers and what are they afraid of?

   A. Patriots; ineffective government

   B. Federalists; the loss of liberty

   C. Antifederalists; a strong national government

   D. Loyalists; the loss of property rights

GO ON

Name _____ Date _____

9. Use the quotation to answer the question.

> "My political curiosity . . . leads me to ask, who authorized them to speak the language of 'We, the People,' instead of 'We, the States'?"
>
> —Patrick Henry, June 4, 1788

Which group did Patrick Henry **most likely** side with during the ratification debate?

A. the Loyalists

B. the Federalists

C. the Antifederalists

D. the Constitutionalists

10. What is meant by "the rule of law"?

A. the idea that people are the source of government power

B. the idea that all people, including rulers and leaders, must obey the law

C. the theory that power should be divided among three branches of government

D. the power of the courts to interpret the Constitution and other laws

11. A court decides that the First Amendment permits a journalist to write an article on something the government wants to keep secret. What type of law was **most** involved in the decision?

A. constitutional law

B. common law

C. statutory law

D. administrative law

12. Use the information in the box to answer the question.

> **ART. 85. DESERTION**
>
> (a) Any member of the armed forces who–
>
> (1) without authority goes or remains absent from his unit, organization, or place of duty with intent to remain away therefrom permanently . . . is guilty of desertion.

What is the source of this law?

A. statutory law

B. common law

C. administrative law

D. military law

13. Use the diagram to answer the question.

The diagram above identifies the steps in becoming a U.S. citizen. Which of the following **best** completes the diagram?

A. be interviewed and pass citizenship tests

B. complete a background check

C. receive appointment letter

D. wait five years

14. What does a person born in any U.S. territory automatically become?

A. a native-born citizen

B. a naturalized citizen

C. a permanent resident alien

D. a refugee

15. Why is it important for citizens to pay taxes?

A. to allow the country to start a draft

B. to help citizens become informed voters

C. to make sure that laws are up to date

D. to provide money to pay for government services

16. Use the line graph to answer the question.

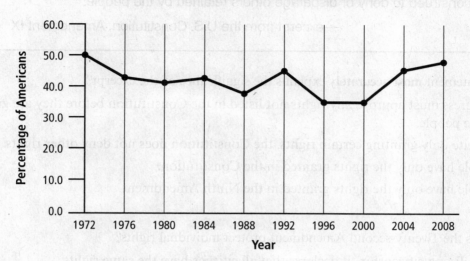

Percentage of Americans Aged 18-24 Who Voted in Presidential Elections

Source: *U.S. Census Bureau*

Which of the following **best** describes the trend of voting among Americans aged 18 to 24 between the 1988 and 2008 presidential elections?

A. a gradual decline, followed by a sharp increase, and then a sharp decline

B. a gradual increase, followed by a gradual decline, and then a sharp decline

C. a sharp decline, followed by a gradual increase, and then a gradual decline

D. a sharp increase, followed by a sharp decline, and then a gradual increase

17. How does registering to vote fulfill a responsibility of citizenship?

A. Registering to vote communicates your opinions to your representatives.

B. Registering to vote makes you eligible to be called for jury duty.

C. Without registering, you cannot express your political views through voting.

D. Without registering, you cannot give money to a political campaign.

GO ON

18. Use the quotation to answer the question.

> "The enumeration in the Constitution, of certain rights, shall not be construed to deny or disparage others retained by the people."
>
> —excerpt from the U.S. Constitution, Amendment IX

Which statement **most accurately** explains the significance of the excerpt?

A. Congress must approve any rights not listed in the Constitution before they are granted to the people.

B. Despite only granting certain rights, the Constitution does not deny other rights.

C. People have only the rights granted in the Constitution.

D. People have only the rights granted in the Ninth Amendment.

19. How does the Twenty-second Amendment protect individual rights?

A. By defining citizenship, it declares that all citizens have the same rights.

B. By granting women the right to vote, it ensures that women have a say in government.

C. By imposing presidential term limits, it prevents one president from gaining too much power.

D. By requiring the direct election of senators, it protects the principle of direct representation.

20. Which of the following **best** describes the purpose of the Bill of Rights?

A. to explain the procedure for amending the Constitution

B. to guarantee freedoms that belong to every citizen

C. to inspire the governments of other nations

D. to limit the rights of individual citizens

21. How does the Fifth Amendment protect an individual's right to own property?

A. by guaranteeing every citizen the right to apply for a home loan

B. by preventing a police search of private property without a warrant

C. by preventing the government from taking private property without fair payment

D. by prohibiting the quartering of soldiers without permission

22. To what age did the Twenty-sixth Amendment lower the voting age?

A. 16

B. 18

C. 21

D. 25

GO ON

23. How did the Twenty-fourth Amendment allow more Americans to vote?

   A. It changed voting laws, which meant that non-U.S. citizens were able to vote.

   B. It outlawed poll taxes, which many states used to prevent poor Americans from voting.

   C. It prevented grandfather clauses, which many states used to prevent women from voting.

   D. It required literacy tests, which meant that Americans became better educated about voting.

24. Use the quotation to answer the question.

   > "It is emphatically [definitely] the province [role] and duty of the Judicial Department to say what the law is. . . . If two laws conflict with each other, the Courts must decide on the operation of each."
   >
   > —Chief Justice John Marshall, *Marbury* v. *Madison*, 1803

   According to the Supreme Court, which branch of government has the power and responsibility to interpret the law?

   A. executive

   B. judicial

   C. legislative

   D. state legislature

GO ON

25. Use the map to answer the question.

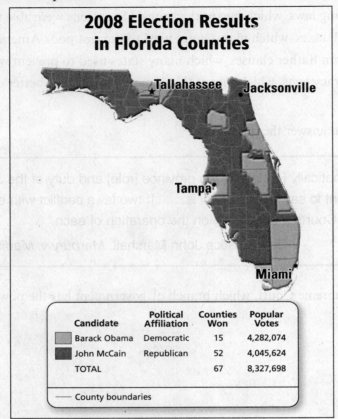

**2008 Election Results
in Florida Counties**

Candidate	Political Affiliation	Counties Won	Popular Votes
Barack Obama	Democratic	15	4,282,074
John McCain	Republican	52	4,045,624
TOTAL		67	8,327,698

—— County boundaries

Which of the Florida cities indicated on the map is located in a county won by the Republican candidate?

A. Jacksonville

B. Miami

C. Tallahassee

D. Tampa

26. Which of the following statements about the Democratic Party is **most accurate**?

A. It is more likely to support reducing the power of the federal government.

B. Its members are said to be more conservative.

C. Its members are said to be more liberal.

D. Its members generally believe state and local government should run social programs.

27. Which is the correct description of a party platform?

A. It is a place where political candidates make speeches.

B. It is a statement that outlines views on issues.

C. It is determined by means of a primary election.

D. It is held after the nominating convention.

GO ON

28. Which question would a citizen want to ask to determine whether a lobbyist is working on behalf of the public interest?

    A. Has the lobbyist worked as a public official before?

    B. How long has the person been a lobbyist?

    C. How much is the lobbyist being paid?

    D. What organization hired the lobbyist?

29. Which is a main purpose of public opinion polls?

    A. analyzing citizen support for a law

    B. getting a law passed

    C. interpreting a newly passed law

    D. opposing a law

30. "Everybody's doing it" is the new slogan for a campaign encouraging people to vote. What propaganda technique is being used?

    A. bandwagon

    B. glittering generalities

    C. name calling

    D. plain-folks appeal

31. You want to get a law passed requiring radon detectors in all houses. What type of group would you **most likely** organize to help reach that goal?

    A. city council

    B. focus group

    C. interest group

    D. political party

32. Which debate during the Constitutional Convention is most related to recent controversy over the USA PATRIOT Act?

    A. distributing power between the state and national governments

    B. ensuring popular sovereignty

    C. guaranteeing individual rights

    D. having a unicameral or bicameral legislature

33. Which of the following issues would **most likely** be a foreign policy matter?

    A. balancing the federal budget

    B. negotiating a treaty with Mexico

    C. raising the retirement age for Social Security

    D. revising neighborhood zoning restrictions

34. Use the table to answer the question.

Organization	Purpose
United Nations	?

Which of the following **best** completes the table?

A. to promote peaceful coexistence and worldwide cooperation

B. to protect member countries from North America and Europe

C. to resolve international legal disputes

D. to supervise and set rules for international trade

35. Why might a citizen oppose the U.S. government's involvement with the United Nations?

A. Because the UN does not give each member country a vote in the General Assembly, UN membership may lead to greater conflict.

B. Because the UN does not have a permanent army, U.S. military forces may become involved in action taken against an aggressor country.

C. Because the United States does not pay a share of UN operating costs, it does not have a say in the General Assembly.

D. Because the United States is not a permanent member of the Security Council, it may not have much influence on UN decisions.

36. How did President Washington respond to the war between Great Britain and France in 1793?

A. by establishing an international alliance to end the conflict

B. by forming an alliance with France

C. by forming an alliance with Great Britain

D. by practicing isolationism and issuing the Neutrality Proclamation

37. Which of the following comparisons is correct?

A. Direct democracies have always been more common than oligarchies.

B. An autocracy might be a monarchy or a dictatorship.

C. In a theocracy, the people have more power than they do in a representative democracy.

D. Socialism and direct democracy are often combined in the same government.

38. Which of the following statements is true of the British Parliament?

A. It is unicameral.

B. Like the U.S. Congress, it is made up of representatives from the states.

C. The head of the government is the prime minister.

D. It is controlled directly by the queen or king.

39. Use the quotation to answer the question.

> ". . . shall have Power To lay and collect Taxes, Duties, Imposts, and Excises, to pay the Debts and provide for the common Defense and general Welfare of the United States . . . to borrow Money . . . to regulate Commerce . . . to coin Money . . ."
>
> —U.S. Constitution, Article I, Section 8

To which branch of the government does the quotation refer?

A. judicial

B. presidential

C. legislative

D. executive

40. Which level of government could pass a law changing the age at which people can marry?

A. state

B. federal

C. county

D. city

41. Use the quotation to answer the question.

> "Why don't they pass a constitutional amendment prohibiting anybody from learning anything? If it works as well as prohibition did, in five years Americans would be the smartest race of people on Earth."
>
> —Will Rogers, "How to Spend It," *Tulsa Daily World*, January 4, 1925

To what was Will Rogers referring?

A. the success of prohibition

B. the right to a public education as guaranteed by the Twenty-first Amendment

C. the importance of being able to easily amend the U.S. Constitution

D. the failure of the Eighteenth Amendment to stop alcohol consumption

42. What term refers to redrawing congressional district boundaries to favor a particular political party?

A. gerrymandering

B. censure

C. impeachment

D. apportionment

43. Use the diagram to answer the question.

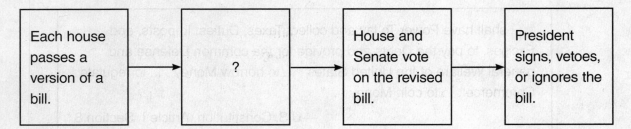

The diagram above summarizes part of the process of how a bill becomes a federal law. Which sentence fills in the second box correctly?

   A. The bill is assigned to a subcommittee.

   B. The president submits his or her recommendations for improvement.

   C. Amendments are added to make the two bills identical.

   D. A conference committee merges the two bills.

44. Of the following, what may happen following a guilty verdict in a criminal case?

   A. A U.S. Court of Appeals asks to review the case.

   B. The criminal case becomes a civil case.

   C. The defendant appeals the case to a higher court.

   D. The U.S. Supreme Court automatically reviews the case.

45. Why do some states prefer the Missouri Plan for choosing judges?

   A. It requires all candidates for judgeships to pass a qualifying test.

   B. It ensures that people who funded the governor's campaign are disqualified.

   C. It combines appointment of judges with election of judges.

   D. It guarantees that only qualified judges can serve for life.

46. Like the U.S. Constitution, the Florida Constitution establishes which of the following?

   A. three branches of government

   B. small claims courts

   C. the right to form treaties with foreign governments

   D. delegated powers

GO ON

47. Use the quotation to answer the question.

> "The way to have good and safe government is not to trust it all to one, but to divide it among the many, distributing to everyone exactly the functions in which he is competent."
>
> —Thomas Jefferson, letter to Joseph C. Cabell, 1816

How does this quote support the idea of different obligations for state and local governments?

A. State governments are more reliable than local governments for providing a city with services.

B. Different levels of government can provide the same services equally well.

C. Local governments can offer a wider range of services to people living nearby.

D. Different levels of government can provide separate services more easily and efficiently.

48. Which official is the top law enforcement official at the county level of government?

A. sheriff

B. mayor

C. county commissioner

D. police commissioner

STOP

Test 2

1. The Founding Fathers divided the power to make, enforce, and interpret laws between the legislative, executive, and judicial branches of government. What might have happened if they had given all of these powers to the executive branch?

   A. The balance of power among the different branches would make government more efficient.

   B. The president could have grown too powerful, leading to tyranny.

   C. Congress would have had more occasions to override presidential vetoes.

   D. Supreme Court justices would have had to strike down more laws as unconstitutional.

2. How did the English Bill of Rights influence delegates to the Constitutional Convention?

   A. It was submitted as a model for the new constitution.

   B. It spelled out the proper role for the legislative branch as the representative of the people.

   C. It had established a number of rights that the delegates wished to guarantee in the new constitution.

   D. It was the first document to limit the power of the monarch.

3. Use the quotation to answer the question.

   > "Every thing that is right or natural pleads for separation. The blood of the slain, the weeping voice of nature cries, 'TIS TIME TO PART. Even the distance at which the Almighty hath placed England and America, is a strong and natural proof, that the authority of the one, over the other, was never the design of Heaven."
   >
   > —Thomas Paine, *Common Sense*, 1776

   What is Thomas Paine trying to win support for?

   A. the separation of natural rights from legal rights

   B. the separation of powers between state and federal governments

   C. the separation of powers between the three branches of government

   D. the separation of the colonies from Great Britain

4. Why were colonists outraged by taxes imposed by the British government?

   A. because they were denied trials by a jury of their peers

   B. because they had no representation in Parliament

   C. because they made British paper products less expensive

   D. because they had to house British soldiers

5. Use the diagram to answer the question.

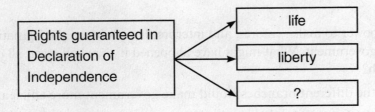

Which of the following correctly completes the diagram?

A. freedom of speech

B. freedom of religion

C. freedom to own property

D. pursuit of happiness

6. Which of the following might have caused people to oppose the Articles of Confederation?

A. Congress had the power to collect taxes.

B. Congress could not pay the soldiers who fought in the Revolutionary War.

C. Congress controlled trade between the states.

D. Congress granted too much power to the executive branch.

7. Use the quotation to answer the question.

"We the People of the United States, in Order to form a more perfect Union, establish Justice, insure domestic Tranquility, provide for the common defense, promote the general Welfare, and secure the Blessings of Liberty to ourselves and our Posterity, do ordain and establish this Constitution for the United States of America."

In which document is this statement found?

A. the Bill of Rights

B. the Preamble of the Constitution

C. the Mayflower Compact

D. *The Federalist Papers*

8. How does the system of checks and balances reinforce the separation of powers?

A. by giving each branch of government powers to limit the other branches

B. by dividing the government duties among three branches

C. by defining the roles of each branch of government in three separate articles

D. by dividing power between the national and state levels of government

9. Why did Antifederalists want a bill of rights in the Constitution?

    A. to list their rights

    B. to protect their rights

    C. to prevent ratification of the Constitution

    D. to argue with Federalists

10. Use the table to answer the question.

Congressional Bills Vetoed, 1981–2008

President	Regular Vetoes	Pocket Vetoes	Total Vetoes	Overridden
Ronald Reagan	39	39	78	9
George H.W. Bush	29	15	44	1
William Clinton	36	1	37	2
George W. Bush	12	0	12	4
Source: *U.S. Senate Library*				

Which constitutional principle does the information in the table illustrate?

    A. social contract

    B. popular sovereignty

    C. federal supremacy

    D. checks and balances

11. Use the information in the box to answer the question.

"Army General Sentenced to Three Years for Killing Civilians"

"Former Senator Convicted of Money Laundering"

"Local Sheriff Arrested for Drunk Driving"

Which constitutional principle is best expressed by these headlines?

    A. individual rights

    B. majority rule

    C. rule of law

    D. minority rights

12. Consider this situation: A man enters an electronics store and points a gun at the store clerk. He demands all of the cash in the register and flees the scene with $3600. What type of law has been violated?

   A. criminal law

   B. military law

   C. common law

   D. civil law

13. Which of the following **best** defines the term *citizen*?

   A. an individual who exercises political authority over a group of people

   B. an individual who is able to vote in elections

   C. a legally recognized member of a country

   D. a person who is loyal to and proud of his or her country

14. Why should citizens know and understand the law?

   A. so that they can break it

   B. so that they can change it

   C. so that they can ignore it

   D. so that they can obey it

15. Why is attending school considered a civic duty?

   A. Educated citizens are vital to the success of our democracy.

   B. The more education a person has, the more money he or she is likely to earn.

   C. School districts depend on having a certain number of students.

   D. Today's high-tech society needs educated employees.

GO ON

16. Use the bar graph to answer the question.

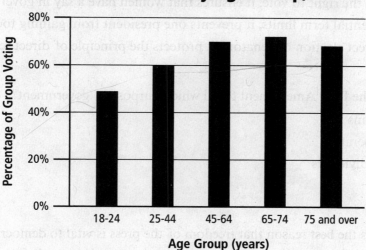

Voter Turnout by Age Group, 2008

Source: *U.S. Census Bureau*

Which age group had the lowest voter turnout?

A. 18 to 24 years

B. 25 to 44 years

C. 45 to 64 years

D. 65 to 74 years

17. Which amendment protects Americans from unreasonable searches and seizures?

A. First Amendment

B. Fourth Amendment

C. Sixth Amendment

D. Thirteenth Amendment

18. The First Amendment protects freedom of speech, but there are some limits to free-speech rights. Why are some forms of speech not protected?

A. because they are expressed in writing

B. because they could cause physical harm to others

C. because they criticize the government

D. because they support different religious views

19. How does the Seventeenth Amendment protect individual rights?

   A. By defining citizenship, it declares that all citizens have the same rights.

   B. By granting women the right to vote, it ensures that women have a say in government.

   C. By imposing presidential term limits, it prevents one president from gaining too much power.

   D. By requiring the direct election of senators, it protects the principle of direct representation.

20. Rights such as those in the First Amendment fulfill which purpose of government?

   A. to guarantee freedoms

   B. to help people cooperate

   C. to limit rights of individuals

   D. to provide services

21. Which of the following is the **best** reason that freedom of the press is vital to democracy?

   A. Freedom of the press allows newspapers to print anything they want.

   B. Freedom of the press allows people to express opinions about government.

   C. Without freedom of the press, the government would be a dictatorship.

   D. Without freedom of the press, there would be few news outlets.

22. Which amendment to the Constitution might the U.S. Supreme Court have relied on when it struck down the death penalty for minors?

   A. First Amendment

   B. Fifth Amendment

   C. Eighth Amendment

   D. Ninth Amendment

23. Use the quotation to answer the question.

> "The right of citizens of the United States to vote shall not be denied or abridged by the United States or by any State on account of sex."
>
> —excerpt from the U.S. Constitution

To which group did this amendment grant the right to vote?

   A. African Americans

   B. land-owning men

   C. Native Americans

   D. women

GO ON

24. Use the quotation to answer the question.

> "This case has shown that punch card balloting machines can produce an unfortunate number of ballots which are not punched in a clean, complete way by the voter. After the current counting, it is likely legislative bodies nationwide will examine ways to improve the mechanisms and machinery for voting."
>
> —*Bush* v. *Gore*, 2000

How did the Supreme Court expect *Bush* v. *Gore* to affect voting practices in the United States?

A. Fewer people would turn out to vote.

B. More people would sign up for absentee ballots.

C. More states would use punch card balloting.

D. States would improve voting methods.

25. Use the table to answer the question.

2008 U.S. Presidential Election Results			
Candidate	**Political Affiliation**	**Electoral Votes**	**Popular Votes**
Barack Obama	Democratic	365	66,882,230
John McCain	Republican	173	58,343,671
TOTAL		538	125,225,901
Source: *CNN*			

How many more electoral votes did the Democratic candidate win than the Republican candidate?

A. 173

B. 192

C. 365

D. 538

26. Which of the following statements about the Republican Party is **most accurate**?

A. It is more likely to support increasing the power of the federal government.

B. Its members are said to be more conservative.

C. Its members are said to be more liberal.

D. Its members generally believe social programs should be run by the federal government.

GO ON ▶

27. What is the **most important** thing that a political debate can teach a voter about a candidate?

A. how much support the candidate already has

B. what kind of television personality the candidate has

C. where the candidate stands on certain issues

D. whether the candidate is comfortable on camera

28. What would be the **most effective** way for a special-interest group to try to influence the outcome of a presidential election?

A. to conduct a public opinion poll

B. to hire a lobbyist

C. to hold a primary election

D. to run television advertisements

29. What is the **best** reason that press releases from a politician or a government agency are not always the best source of public information about an issue?

A. They are not covered by news outlets.

B. They give too much detail to be useful.

C. They may be released too late to be useful.

D. They may present only one point of view about an issue.

30. In a speech, a government official tries to increase support for a budget proposal by making an emotional appeal to liberty and equality. Which propaganda technique is being used?

A. bandwagon

B. card stacking

C. glittering generalities

D. testimonial

31. What level of government would you **most likely** contact to address a community issue?

A. local government

B. state government

C. federal government

D. international government

GO ON

32. Use the table to answer the question.

Important Issues for the President and Congress to Address, January 2011				
	Extremely Important	**Very Important**	**Moderately Important**	**Not That Important/ No Opinion**
Economy	63%	32%	4%	2%
Unemployment	54%	34%	9%	3%
Health care	52%	31%	12%	5%
Federal budget deficit	52%	33%	12%	2%
Social Security and Medicare	47%	35%	14%	4%
Education	47%	36%	13%	4%
Terrorism	45%	35%	17%	3%
Taxes	41%	36%	21%	2%
Situation in Afghanistan	36%	36%	26%	3%
Situation in Iraq	34%	30%	29%	7%
Energy policy	33%	37%	26%	5%
Illegal immigration	32%	29%	28%	11%
Gun policy	24%	19%	27%	30%
Source: *CNN Opinion Research Poll, January 21–23, 2011*				

Which of the following issues is considered "extremely important" by the highest percentage of Americans polled?

A. economy

B. health care

C. terrorism

D. unemployment

33. Which of the following issues would **most likely** be a domestic policy matter?

A. declaring war

B. meeting with the prime minister of Great Britain

C. revising campaign finance laws

D. supervising democratic elections in Iraq

34. Use the table to answer the question.

Organization	Purpose
NATO	?

Which of the following **best** completes the table?

A. to promote peaceful coexistence and worldwide cooperation

B. to protect member countries in North America and Europe

C. to resolve international legal disputes

D. to supervise and set rules for international trade

35. How is the Peace Corps different from many other U.S. government agencies working with foreign countries?

A. American citizens volunteer to be a part of the Peace Corps.

B. Members of the Peace Corps must also be members of the diplomatic corps.

C. The Peace Corps allows voters to choose where it sends workers.

D. The Peace Corps only works on technology projects.

36. What policy did Woodrow Wilson attempt to follow in 1914 when World War I began?

A. dollar diplomacy

B. interventionism

C. neutrality

D. protectionism

37. Which of the following systems proposes that society should organize and control the means of production for the welfare of all?

A. communism

B. monarchy

C. socialism

D. direct democracy

38. What sort of government was established by the Articles of Confederation?

A. a union in which some states had more power than others

B. a loose association of states

C. a firm union of states

D. a federal arrangement with a strong central government

GO ON

39. Use the table to answer the question.

Legislative branch	Passes bills that become the law of the land
Executive branch	?
Judicial branch	Interprets the meaning of laws and punishes lawbreakers

Which phrase completes the table?

A. Appoints officials and administers agencies to carry out the laws

B. Rules on the constitutionality of laws

C. Enforces laws not under another jurisdiction

D. Creates legislatures to develop new laws

40. If a northern state's governor has a dispute with Canada over the location of the U.S.-Canada border, which of the following is prohibited by law?

A. meeting with the Canadian prime minister

B. refusing to buy Canadian products

C. declaring war on Canada

D. threatening a tourism boycott of Canada

41. Of the following, what is one thing that both the federal government and state governments are allowed by law to do?

A. raise armies

B. negotiate treaties

C. collect taxes

D. administer elections

GO ON

42. Use the diagram to answer the question.

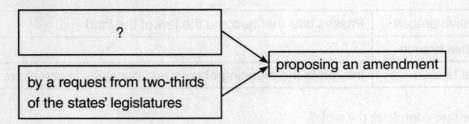

This diagram shows two methods for proposing an amendment to the U.S. Constitution. What method correctly fills in the top box?

A. by a request from a majority of the states' governors

B. by a two-thirds vote in both houses of the U.S. Congress

C. by a petition from five of the U.S. Supreme Court justices

D. by a request from at least 26 state conventions

43. Which of the following may happen after the Supreme Court declares a law unconstitutional?

A. Congress can over-rule the Supreme Court by a two-thirds majority.

B. The president can propose an amendment that makes the law constitutional.

C. Congress can pass a new law that addresses the Supreme Court's concerns.

D. The president can over-rule the Supreme Court.

44. What is an ordinance?

A. a regulation that governs a community

B. a local law that conflicts with state law

C. a state law amended to fit local requirements

D. a basic plan for a local government unit

45. What are the three main levels of federal courts?

A. district courts, courts of appeals, and the U.S. Supreme Court

B. city courts, state courts, and the U.S. Supreme Court

C. mayor's court, city court, and federal court

D. district courts, magistrate courts, and the U.S. Supreme Court

GO ON

46. Use the quotation to answer the question.

> "There are two things you don't want to see being made—sausage and legislation."

This quotation has been attributed to Otto von Bismarck, Germany's chancellor from 1871 to 1890. When people quote this line, what do you think they are saying?

A. Law-making can be messy and unpleasant.

B. Law-making should be done in secret.

C. Legislation is made up of many pieces, like sausage.

D. Legislation should be left to politicians.

47. What is one way in which the U.S. and Florida constitutions differ?

A. The Florida governor is allowed to create new cabinet positions, but the U.S. president cannot.

B. The Florida Constitution requires the governor to be appointed by the legislature, in contrast to the popular election of the U.S. president.

C. The U.S. Constitution requires election of cabinet secretaries, but Florida's constitution does not.

D. Florida identifies specific cabinet positions that must be part of the executive branch, but the U.S. Constitution does not.

48. Selling lottery tickets is a common way of raising money for education. If a majority of Floridians decided they wanted to end the lottery, to which division of the government would they complain?

A. their county commissioners' courts

B. the state

C. their city council

D. their school superintendents

Name _____ Date _____

Test 3

1. Which Enlightenment thinker argued that all people were born equal and had natural rights to life, liberty, and property?

 A. Jean-Jacques Rousseau

 B. Baron de Montesquieu

 C. Thomas Hobbes

 D. John Locke

2. Use the quotation to answer the question.

> "No freeman shall be taken, imprisoned, . . . or in any other way destroyed . . . except by the lawful judgement of his peers or by the law of the land."
>
> — excerpt from Magna Carta

 Which statement best expresses how Magna Carta shaped the colonists' views of government?

 A. They supported three branches of government.

 B. They believed that citizens should be able to petition the government for changes in laws.

 C. They expected government to protect free speech and property rights.

 D. They believed leaders should obey the law and that citizens had a right to trial by jury.

3. Use the information in the box to answer the question.

> **Events Leading to American Independence**
> 1. The Declaration of Independence is issued.
> 2. British Parliament passes Tea Act.
> 3. Boston Tea Party staged to protest British policies.
> 4. First battles of the American Revolution are fought.

 What is the correct sequence of events?

 A. 2, 1, 4, 3

 B. 4, 2, 3, 1

 C. 2, 3, 4, 1

 D. 1, 2, 4, 3

GO ON

4. The Declaration of Independence lists a number of offenses committed by the British king against the American colonists. Which of the following offenses refers to a protection first established by Magna Carta?

   A. For cutting off our Trade with all parts of the world

   B. For imposing Taxes on us without our Consent

   C. For depriving us in many cases, of the benefits of Trial by Jury

   D. For transporting us beyond Seas to be tried for pretended offence

5. According to the Declaration of Independence, what is the main purpose of government?

   A. to provide for common defense and promote the general welfare

   B. to create a strong national government

   C. to protect the interests of the states

   D. to protect citizens' rights to life, liberty, and the pursuit of happiness

6. Use the diagram to answer the question.

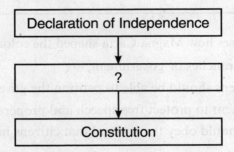

   Which term **correctly** completes the diagram?

   A. Magna Carta

   B. Mayflower Compact

   C. Articles of Confederation

   D. Bill of Rights

GO ON

7. Use the quotation to answer the question.

> "We the People of the United States, in Order to form a more perfect Union, establish Justice, insure domestic Tranquility, provide for the common defense, promote the general Welfare, and secure the Blessings of Liberty to ourselves and our Posterity [future generations], do ordain and establish this Constitution for the United States of America."
>
> —excerpt from the Preamble of the U.S. Constitution

What does the phrase "to ourselves and our Posterity" suggest about the Founding Fathers' goals?

A. They wanted to create a lasting government that future Americans would benefit from.

B. They were willing to sacrifice their liberty for the benefit of their children.

C. They aimed to create a strong government, independent of the will of the people.

D. They wanted to create a social contract that future Americans could not break.

8. Use the diagram to answer the question.

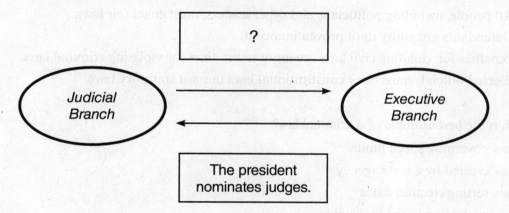

Which of the following completes the diagram?

A. The Supreme Court can declare executive acts unconstitutional.

B. The Supreme Court can appoint federal judges.

C. The Supreme Court can declare acts of Congress unconstitutional.

D. The Supreme Court can grant reprieves and pardons for federal crimes.

9. What did Federalists and Antifederalists disagree most strongly about?

A. a strong national government

B. creating a system of checks and balances

C. protecting individual liberties

D. increasing the power of the confederation

GO ON

10. Use these quotations to answer the question.

> "Where-ever law ends, tyranny begins."
>
> —John Locke, *Two Treatises of Government,* 1690
>
> "That in America THE LAW IS KING. For as in absolute governments the King is law, so in free countries the law ought to be King; and there ought to be no other."
>
> —Thomas Paine, *Common Sense,* 1776

Which conclusion about the rule of law is **best supported** by these quotations?

A. The rule of law leads to tyranny.

B. Freedom and the rule of law cannot exist together.

C. People in positions of power must enact fair laws.

D. The rule of law is necessary for limited government.

11. What is one way that the rule of law has influenced the development of the American legal system?

A. All people, including politicians and other leaders, must enact fair laws.

B. Defendants are guilty until proven innocent.

C. Penalties for violating civil laws are more severe than for violating criminal laws.

D. Elected officials must obey constitutional laws but not statutory laws.

12. Which is the **best** example of a criminal law?

A. law governing speed limits

B. law created by a state agency

C. law setting election dates

D. law protecting individual rights

13. Which of the following terms is defined as the legal process of becoming a U.S. citizen?

A. adoption

B. assimilation

C. immigration

D. naturalization

14. Why does the government require qualified 18-year-old males to register for military service?

A. to allow the government to quickly draft them in times of crisis

B. to ensure that they are also registered to vote

C. to provide jobs for more people

D. to provide money to pay for government services

15. Use the diagram to answer the question.

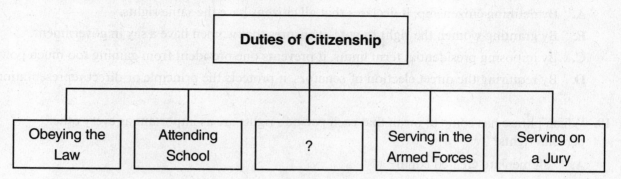

Duties of citizenship are things we must do. Responsibilities of citizenship are things we should do. Which duty of citizenship is missing from the diagram?

A. being informed

B. paying taxes

C. volunteering in the community

D. voting

16. Which of the following is the **most likely** reason that an individual might volunteer with a political campaign?

A. to appear in the media

B. to avoid having to vote

C. to earn money

D. to influence the election

17. Use the quotation to answer the question.

> "In all criminal prosecutions, the accused shall enjoy the right to a speedy and public trial, by an impartial jury."
>
> —excerpt from the U.S. Constitution

Which amendment is this quotation from?

A. First Amendment

B. Fourth Amendment

C. Sixth Amendment

D. Thirteenth Amendment

GO ON

18. How does the Fourteenth Amendment protect individual rights?

    A. By defining citizenship, it declares that all citizens have the same rights.

    B. By granting women the right to vote, it ensures that women have a say in government.

    C. By imposing presidential term limits, it prevents one president from gaining too much power.

    D. By requiring the direct election of senators, it protects the principle of direct representation.

19. Which phrase has come to mean that each person's rights are as important as every other person's rights?

    A. "all men are created equal"

    B. "all power is vested in, and derived from, the people"

    C. "Life, Liberty, and the pursuit of Happiness"

    D. "We the People"

20. Use the photograph to answer the question.

© Joe Raedle/Getty Images

What First Amendment right are the people in this photograph expressing?

    A. freedom of assembly

    B. freedom of the press

    C. freedom of religion

    D. right to privacy

21. Which of the following statements **best** describes an aspect of American government?

    A. The press can print anything it wants.

    B. The president has the power to establish a national religion.

    C. Citizens have the right to protect their reputations against lies.

    D. Congress can decide which citizens may vote.

22. How did the Fourteenth Amendment's due process clause extend the Bill of Rights?

    A. by claiming additional rights not mentioned in the Bill of Rights

    B. by extending the right to vote to all U.S. citizens

    C. by granting full citizenship to African Americans

    D. by preventing states from denying rights granted in the Bill of Rights

23. Use the quotation to answer the question.

> "In practically all jurisdictions, there are rights granted to adults which are withheld from juveniles. . . . Under our Constitution, the condition of being a boy [or girl] does not justify a kangaroo court [an unfair trial]."
>
> —Justice Abe Fortas, *In re Gault,* 1967

According to the Supreme Court, why should juveniles have the same right to a fair trial that adults have?

    A. Being a child is not a good enough reason to deny them this right.

    B. Juveniles should not be tried for their crimes at all.

    C. Since they are denied other rights, they deserve this one.

    D. The U.S. Constitution does not protect juvenile delinquents.

24. Which Supreme Court decision **most** helped overturn the "separate but equal" doctrine?

    A. *Brown* v. *Board of Education*

    B. *Hazelwood* v. *Kuhlmeier*

    C. *Miranda* v. *Arizona*

    D. *Plessy* v. *Ferguson*

GO ON

25. Use the table to answer the question.

2008 Presidential Election Results in Florida			
Candidate	**Political Affiliation**	**Counties Won**	**Popular Votes**
Barack Obama	Democratic	15	4,282,074
John McCain	Republican	52	4,045,624
TOTAL		67	8,327,698
Source: *CNN*			

What percentage of Florida counties did the Democratic candidate win?

A. 22 percent

B. 49 percent

C. 51 percent

D. 78 percent

26. Which of the following statements about the Republican Party is **most accurate**?

A. It is more likely to support increasing the power of the federal government.

B. It is more likely to support reducing the power of the federal government.

C. Its members are said to be more liberal.

D. Its members generally believe the federal government should run social programs.

27. Which of the following would be the **best** source for accurate information about a candidate's experience and qualifications?

A. an interest group's concealed propaganda

B. a letter to the editor published in the local newspaper

C. a speech made by an opposing candidate

D. an unbiased voter guide written by an independent group

28. Which of the following is the **least common** method lobbyists use to try to influence public policy?

A. donating money to political parties

B. helping write legislation

C. meeting with individual voters

D. testifying at public hearings

GO ON

29. Which source would be **most likely** to provide a thorough and balanced analysis of political issues?

    A. an article in an independent political journal

    B. a call-in radio show

    C. an interest group's campaign ad

    D. text messages from a friend

30. A politician has a picture taken of him mowing the yard. Which propaganda technique is being used?

    A. glittering generalities

    B. name calling

    C. plain-folks appeal

    D. testimonial

31. A state legislature fails to pass a law because the two houses cannot agree on a compromise bill. How can citizens get the law passed without the legislature's help?

    A. approve an initiative

    B. approve a petition

    C. approve a recall

    D. approve a referendum

32. Opponents of the USA PATRIOT Act would **most likely** argue that it violates which part of the U.S. Constitution?

    A. freedom of speech

    B. guarantee of a republican form of government

    C. protection against unreasonable searches

    D. right to bear arms

33. Which of the following issues would **most likely** be a foreign policy matter?

    A. cutting the federal income tax rate

    B. drafting a law to increase unemployment benefits

    C. providing assistance to a needy family in Miami

    D. providing assistance to an orphanage in Bangladesh

34. Use the table to answer the question.

Organization	Purpose
?	to resolve international legal disputes

Which of the following **best** completes the table?

A. International Court of Justice

B. NATO

C. United Nations

D. World Trade Organization

35. Why did the United States join NATO?

A. It wanted allies to assist with its efforts to seek out terrorists in Afghanistan.

B. It wanted allies to oppose aggression by the Soviet Union and other communist nations.

C. It wanted to eliminate trade barriers between the United States, Canada, and Mexico.

D. It wanted to protect future generations against war and to promote cooperation among all nations.

36. What was the United States' approach to fighting communism in the late 1940s called?

A. containment

B. détente

C. dollar diplomacy

D. limited war

37. Use the quotation to answer the question.

> "Western policies must encourage the evolution of the Soviet Union toward an open society. This task . . . will require a sweeping vision. Let me share with you my vision: I see a Western Hemisphere of democratic, prosperous nations, no longer threatened by a Cuba or a Nicaragua armed by Moscow."
>
> —President George H. W. Bush, May 12, 1989

To which twentieth-century situation was Bush referring?

A. the end of communism in the Soviet Union

B. the development of direct democracy in Russia

C. the failure of representative democracy in Europe

D. the emergence of new Stalinist monarchies

38. Which statement about monarchies is correct?

    A. Jordan is the world's only true monarchy.

    B. Saudi Arabia is a constitutional monarchy.

    C. The monarchs of the United Kingdom have limited power.

    D. There are more monarchies than there were 100 years ago.

39. From which of the following courts is there no appeal?

    A. U.S. Court of Appeals

    B. U.S. Supreme Court

    C. U.S. District Court

    D. U.S. High Court

40. Use the table to answer the question.

Type of Power	Definition
delegated powers	powers given to the federal government
?	powers held by the states that are not given specifically to the federal government
concurrent powers	powers shared by the federal and state governments

Which phrase completes the table?

    A. judicial powers

    B. statutory powers

    C. legislated powers

    D. reserved powers

41. Consider this situation: A U.S. senator has been in office for more than 40 years, having been re-elected many times. He begins to make policy decisions that favor special interest groups over the interests of his constituents. Of the following, which is most likely to be a topic of discussion among his constituents?

    A. medical exams for candidates

    B. term limits for candidates

    C. minimum age requirements for candidates

    D. cultural sensitivity training for candidates

42. What is the term for powers shared by both state and federal governments?

    A. declared powers

    B. concurrent powers

    C. relegated powers

    D. representative powers

43. What does it mean to ratify an amendment to the Constitution?

   A. revise it

   B. approve it

   C. reject it

   D. send it to a committee

44. Why does the executive branch include many independent agencies and regulatory commissions?

   A. The U.S. Constitution limits the number of cabinet departments that can be created.

   B. Many of the executive branch's duties do not fit the 15 established departments.

   C. The cabinet departments cannot be divided into smaller units.

   D. The federal bureaucracy is prohibited from performing many necessary tasks.

45. Which of the following statements is true regarding the law-making process at the local level?

   A. County governments usually make laws by approving the sheriff's proposals.

   B. At a town meeting, people can vote directly on various issues.

   C. Townships are gaining more law-making power as more people move to suburbs.

   D. Each state has 10 to 15 school districts that pass laws regarding education.

46. Use the chart to answer the question.

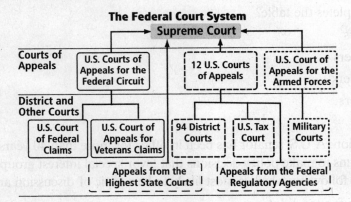

How would appeals from the U.S. Court of Appeals for Veterans Claims reach the Supreme Court?

   A. through the U.S. Court of Appeals for the Armed Forces

   B. through one of the 94 U.S. Courts of Appeals

   C. through the military courts

   D. through one of the U.S. Courts of Appeals for the Federal Circuit

47. What is one way that the amendments to the Florida Constitution are different from those for the U.S. Constitution?

   A. They are listed at the end of the document.

   B. They are made to the text of the official document.

   C. They can only be proposed by Florida citizen.

   D. Explanatory notes are not allowed.

48. Use the quotation to answer the question.

> "Gathered here tonight are some of Florida's most dedicated public servants. All of you rank among the best and brightest minds our state has to offer.
>
>   On behalf of tens of thousands of Florida employers: Thank you for taking swift action to help our economy on this opening day of the 2010 Legislative Session. . . . I look forward to signing this important legislation as soon as it comes to my desk."
>
> —Charlie Crist, former Florida governor, March, 2010

This quotation is **most likely** from which of the following sources?

   A. the governor's budget proposal

   B. the governor's inaugural address

   C. the governor's State of the State address

   D. the governor's audit

Test 4

1. Use the quotation to answer the question.

> "To secure these rights, Governments are instituted among Men, deriving their just powers from the consent of the governed."
>
> —excerpt from the Declaration of Independence

Which Enlightenment idea is expressed in this statement?

A. Baron de Montesquieu's theory of separation of power

B. John Locke's idea of the social contract

C. Jean-Jacques Rousseau's theory of divine right

D. James Madison's view of individual liberty

2. Use the quotation to answer the question.

> "We, whose names are underwritten . . . solemnly and mutually . . . covenant [agree to] and combine ourselves together into a civil Body Politick [government], for our better Ordering and Preservation."
>
> —excerpt from the Mayflower Compact

This part of the Mayflower Compact is an example of how the colonists put which of the following into practice?

A. social contract theory

B. common law

C. statute

D. checks and balances

3. Which newspaper headline reports a British action that angered colonists and led to the writing of the Declaration of Independence?

A. "Boycott British Goods!"

B. "The King Grants Independence!"

C. "British Taxes: Unfair!"

D. "Angry Colonists Dump Tea!"

4. Use the timeline to answer the question.

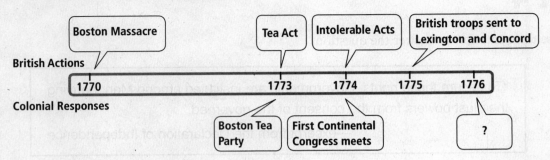

Which event correctly completes the timeline?

A. Articles of Confederation

B. Bill of Rights

C. Constitution

D. Declaration of Independence

5. Use the quotation to answer the question.

> "We hold these truths to be self-evident, that all men are created equal, that they are endowed by their Creator with certain unalienable Rights, that among these are Life, Liberty, and the pursuit of Happiness. That to secure these rights, Governments are instituted among Men, deriving their just powers from the consent of the governed . . ."
>
> —excerpt from the Declaration of Independence

According to this excerpt, how does the source of natural rights compare to the source of government power?

A. Natural rights come from the government; government power comes from the people

B. Natural rights come from God; government power comes from the people.

C. Natural rights come from the government; government power comes from God.

D. Natural rights come from God; government power comes from God.

GO ON

6. Use the table to answer the question.

Weaknesses in the Articles of Confederation

Weakness	Effect
No power to enforce laws	The national government was dependent on the states to enforce laws
No executive branch	No way to enforce laws; no way to coordinate the work of the national government
No judicial branch	No way to interpret laws or settle disputes between states

How did these weaknesses impact the writing of the Constitution?

A. The Founding Fathers gave Congress the power to legislate.

B. The Founding Fathers created a government with three branches.

C. The Founding Fathers gave the states the power to interpret national laws?

D. The Founding Fathers created the office of president to settle disputes.

7. According to the Preamble of the Constitution, which of the following are basic purposes of government?

A. provide services, provide laws, and guarantee freedoms

B. establish justice, ensure tranquility, provide for common defense, and promote welfare

C. ensure life, liberty, property, and the pursuit of happiness

D. collect taxes, print money, establish a military, and regulate commerce

8. Use the quotation to answer the question.

> "We the People of the United States, in Order to form a more perfect Union, establish Justice, insure domestic Tranquility, provide for the common defense, promote the general Welfare, and secure the Blessings of Liberty to ourselves and our Posterity [future generations], do ordain and establish this Constitution for the United States of America."
>
> —excerpt from the Preamble of the U.S. Constitution

Which of the following **most clearly** reveals the Founders ideas about the source of government power?

A. "We the People"

B. "a more perfect Union"

C. "this Constitution"

D. "our Posterity"

9. In what way does the power of judicial review act as a check?

   A. Courts can declare presidential acts unconstitutional.

   B. Courts can declare congressional acts unconstitutional.

   C. Courts can declare presidential and congressional acts unconstitutional.

   D. Courts can review acts of other courts.

10. Which of the following is true of the Federalists?

    A. They opposed ratification of the Constitution.

    B. They opposed a strong central government.

    C. They supported the division of the United States into 13 separate countries.

    D. They feared the Articles of Confederation could not keep the country united.

11. Consider this situation: A president of a nation orders lawyers and judges to be put in jail so that he or she can remain in power and not be tried for crimes against the people. What basic principle of American government does this violate?

    A. checks and balances   C. federalism

    B. the rule of law   D. separation of power

12. Use the table to answer the question.

?	Civil Law
• Laws designed to prevent behavior that is harmful to society as a whole • Used to protect against assault, murder, rape, and theft	• Laws that help settle disputes between people • Used to help settle contract disputes, divorce proceedings, and property boundaries

Which of the following correctly completes the missing title in this table?

    A. Criminal Law   C. Military Law

    B. Common Law   D. Constitutional Law

13. Which of the following lists steps of the naturalization process in the correct order, from first to last?

    A. apply for citizenship, take oath of allegiance, interview and pass citizenship tests, apply for a permanent resident visa

    B. apply for a permanent resident visa, apply for citizenship, interview and pass citizenship tests, take oath of allegiance

    C. apply for a permanent resident visa, interview and pass citizenship tests, take oath of allegiance, apply for citizenship

    D. interview and pass citizenship tests, apply for a permanent resident visa, apply for citizenship, take oath of allegiance

GO ON

14. Which of the following are all U.S. citizens required to do?

A. serve on a jury

B. perform community service

C. volunteer for a campaign

D. vote in an election

15. Which duty of citizenship is critical to support government services?

A. obeying the law

B. paying taxes

C. serving on a jury

D. serving in the military

16. Use the table to answer the question.

Percentage of Voting-Age Florida Residents Who Voted	
Year	Percentage
1972	59.0
1976	54.7
1980	55.5
1984	53.3
1988	54.5
1992	55.8
1996	50.7
2000	51.6
2004	56.1
2008	56.5
Source: U.S. Census Bureau	

Which of the following **best** describes the trend of voting among Florida residents since 1996?

A. The percentage of Florida residents who voted has decreased since 1996.

B. The percentage of Florida residents who voted has increased since 1996.

C. The percentage of Florida residents who voted has stayed the same since 1996.

D. The percentage of Florida residents who voted has exceeded the national average since 1996.

Name _____ Date _____

17. What is the **most important** reason for citizens to volunteer for community service projects?

    A. It helps solve problems in the community.

    B. It looks good on a college application.

    C. It raises the community's employment level.

    D. It shows a sense of commitment.

18. Use the quotation to answer the question.

> "Congress shall make no law respecting an establishment of religion, or prohibiting the free exercise thereof; or abridging the freedom of speech, or of the press; or the right of the people peaceably to assemble, and to petition the Government for a redress of grievances."
>
> —excerpt from the U.S. Constitution

Which amendment is this quotation from?

    A. First Amendment

    B. Fourth Amendment

    C. Sixth Amendment

    D. Thirteenth Amendment

19. How do the Ninth and Tenth amendments limit the power of the federal government?

    A. by listing specific rights that belong to the states

    B. by listing specific rights that belong to the people

    C. by preventing the federal government from changing the Constitution

    D. by reserving rights not granted to the federal government for the states and people

20. Which of the following is a limitation of the First Amendment's guarantee of the right to freedom of speech?

    A. People may not criticize the actions of their neighbors.

    B. People may not criticize the government.

    C. People may not deliver a speech in public.

    D. People may not tell lies that might harm another person.

21. Which of the following statements **best** describes how the First Amendment affects religion in the United States?

    A. The government cannot dictate religion.

    B. The government has an official religion.

    C. There can be no religion in the United States.

    D. State employees cannot have a religion.

22. What happened as a result of the Thirteenth Amendment?

    A. African Americans got the right to vote.

    B. All citizens were guaranteed equal protection under the law.

    C. The right to own slaves was extended for 20 years.

    D. Slavery was outlawed in all states and U.S. territories.

23. According to the Fifteenth Amendment, on what basis could citizens no longer be denied the right to vote?

    A. on the basis of employment

    B. on the basis of gender

    C. on the basis of race or color

    D. on the basis of religion

24. Use the quotation to answer the question.

> "Does segregation of children in public schools solely on the basis of race, even though the physical facilities and other 'tangible' factors may be equal, deprive the children of the minority group of equal educational opportunities? We believe that it does."
>
> —Chief Justice Earl Warren, *Brown* v. *Board of Education*, 1954

Why did the Supreme Court decide that the "separate but equal" doctrine in public education was unconstitutional?

    A. They argued that even if physical facilities were equal, segregation in education still denied minority students equal opportunities.

    B. They decided that it was impossible for local school districts to make separate educational facilities equal.

    C. They determined that the development of separate educational facilities was too expensive to continue.

    D. They suggested that it was impossible to tell if separate educational facilities were depriving minority students of equal opportunities.

25. Which of the following statements about the Democratic Party is **most accurate**?

    A. It is more likely to support reducing the power of the federal government.

    B. Its members are said to be more conservative.

    C. Its members generally believe the federal government should run social programs.

    D. Its members generally believe state and local government should run social programs.

GO ON

26. Why is it important to analyze political ads carefully before choosing a candidate?

    A. Political ads are designed to convince you to vote for a candidate and may not present all sides of an issue.

    B. Political ads are usually an afterthought for a campaign and probably do not contain up-to-date information.

    C. Political ads contain only propaganda and lies and should not be a factor when selecting a candidate.

    D. Political ads often present a balanced viewpoint of all issues and therefore can be a good source of information.

27. What is the **most direct** way to use the mass media to promote political change?

    A. by purchasing an advertisement

    B. by staging a political demonstration

    C. by voting

    D. by writing letters to a politician

28. Use the table to answer the question.

Print and Online Newspaper Readership			
Read yesterday…	2006	2008	2010
Any newspaper, including online	43%	39%	37%
In print	38%	30%	26%
Online	9%	13%	17%
Source: *Pew Research Center, 2010*			

How has the percentage of Americans reading newspapers, including in print and online, changed since 2006?

    A. It has decreased from 37 percent to 17 percent.

    B. It has decreased from 38 percent to 26 percent.

    C. It has decreased from 43 percent to 37 percent.

    D. It has increased from 9 percent to 17 percent.

29. Which responsibility of citizenship **most** helps a person detect card stacking?

    A. expressing one's opinions

    B. running for political office

    C. staying well informed

    D. voting

30. A rock star promotes a social services program by telling about how the program helped her family get through hard times. Which propaganda technique is being used?

   A. bandwagon

   B. card stacking

   C. glittering generalities

   D. testimonial

31. A local agency would **most likely** be involved with a decision about which of the following?

   A. enforcing U.S. immigration laws

   B. determining when to interview candidates running for public office

   C. investigating how to pay for a new campus for the state university

   D. restricting the types of businesses in a particular neighborhood

32. Use the bar graph to answer the question.

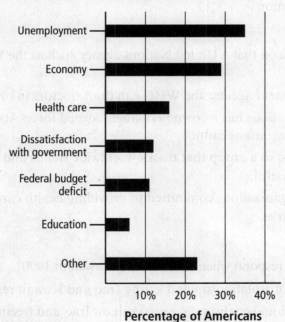

Most Important Problem in the United States Today

Source: *Gallup Poll, February 2011*

What percentage of Americans listed some kind of economic issue as the most important problem facing the United States?

   A. 11%

   B. 29%

   C. 35%

   D. 75%

GO ON

33. Which of the following issues would **most likely** be a domestic policy matter?

    A. attending a meeting of the United Nations

    B. proposing a new policy for funding education

    C. sending military troops to Afghanistan

    D. sending Peace Corps volunteers to Senegal

34. Use the table to answer the question.

Organization	Purpose
?	to supervise and set rules for international trade

Which of the following **best** completes the table?

    A. International Court of Justice

    B. NATO

    C. United Nations

    D. World Trade Organization

35. Which is the **most likely** reason that a United Nations agency such as the World Health Organization (WHO) might be needed?

    A. Because it is a government agency, the WHO can draft doctors in order to save on labor costs.

    B. Because the United Nations has its own permanent armed forces, its agencies are able to go places that other organizations cannot.

    C. Diseases cross borders, so a group that tracks worldwide trends and provides a global perspective could be useful.

    D. There are no other organizations committed to providing health care to underdeveloped countries.

36. How did the United States respond when Iraq invaded Kuwait in 1990?

    A. by following a policy of isolationism and letting Iraq and Kuwait resolve the issue

    B. by leading an international coalition in an assault on Iraq and freeing Kuwait from Iraqi control

    C. by supporting Iraq's right to keep the territory it had claimed

    D. by working through diplomatic channels to negotiate the withdrawal of Iraqi troops from Kuwait

GO ON

37. Consider this situation: In an ancient kingdom, the people were tired of being treated badly by their king. The people of each village got together and chose chiefs to bring their complaints to the king. What kind of government did the villagers demonstrate by their actions?

A. autocracy

B. direct democracy

C. monarchy

D. representative democracy

38. Use the quotation to answer the question.

> "But as the plan of the [Constitutional] convention aims only at a partial union or consolidation, the State governments would clearly retain all the rights of sovereignty which they before had, and which were not, by that act, EXCLUSIVELY delegated to the United States."
>
> —Alexander Hamilton, *Federalist Paper* No. 32

What form of government is being described?

A. confederal

B. unitary

C. parliamentary

D. federal

39. Which of the following describes a unitary system of government?

A. a country in which the central government holds all the power

B. a federal arrangement of central government and states

C. the United States under the Articles of Confederation

D. independent legislatures in several provinces

40. The vice president serves as president if the president dies, leaves office, or is unable to fulfill his or her duties. What other job of the vice president is defined in the Constitution?

A. presiding over the Senate

B. attending funerals in foreign countries

C. representing Washington, D.C., in the Senate

D. negotiating treaties

GO ON

41. The table below describes some of the powers described in the U.S. Constitution.

Type of Power	Definition
delegated powers	powers given to the federal government
reserved powers	powers held by the states that are not given specifically to the federal government
?	powers shared by the federal and state governments

Which phrase completes the table?

A. judicial powers

B. statutory powers

C. legislated powers

D. concurrent powers

42. Which of the following is true of the constitutional amendment process?

A. Three-fourths of the states must ratify proposed amendments.

B. The easy process has allowed hundreds of amendments to be approved.

C. State conventions must vote to ratify amendments.

D. Over half of the original amendments have been repealed.

43. Use the table to answer the question.

Amendment	Time required for ratification	Year ratified
XXIII Washington, D.C., vote	9 months	1961
XXIV Abolition of poll taxes	1 year, 4 months	1964
XXV Presidential succession	1 year, 10 months	1967
XXVI Eighteen-year-old suffrage	3 months	1971
XXVII Regulating congressional pay	203 years	1992

This table shows the length of time between congressional approval and actual ratification of the five most recent amendments to the U.S. Constitution. What conclusion can be drawn from this table?

A. It always takes a long time to ratify amendments.

B. Some amendments have been ratified within a year of their approval.

C. Regulating congressional pay was a topic on which everyone agreed.

D. Ratification is a smooth process.

44. Use the image to answer the question.

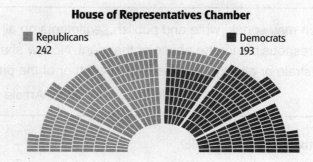

House of Representatives Chamber

Republicans 242   Democrats 193

Which of the following best summarizes the image?

A. Most representatives do not belong to a political party.

B. The House is evenly divided between Republicans, Democrats, and Undecideds.

C. The Republicans have a majority.

D. The Democrats have a two-thirds majority.

45. If a state's citizens start a petition drive to remove the governor from office, what process are the citizens pursuing?

A. initiative

B. referendum

C. impeachment

D. recall

46. What official is in charge of a state's legal business?

A. Chief Justice of the state's Supreme Court

B. governor

C. chief legal counsel of the state

D. attorney general

47. Use the quotation to answer the question.

> "Every person may speak, write and publish sentiments on all subjects
> but shall be responsible for the abuse of that right. No law shall be
> passed to restrain or abridge the liberty of speech or of the press."
>
> —Florida Constitution, Article I, Section 4

What document does this passage resemble?

A. U.S. Constitution, Second Amendment

B. U.S. Constitution, First Amendment

C. Bill of Rights, Fourteenth Amendment

D. Declaration of Independence

48. Consider this situation: A mayor is elected by a city's voters. He appoints people who contributed heavily to his campaign to various positions within city government. The city council objects but can not fire these officials. Which form of city government is described?

A. council-manager plan

B. county commission plan

C. strong-mayor plan

D. mayor-council plan

Name _____ Date _____

Multiple Choice

1. Use the quotation to answer the question.

   > "No freeman shall be taken, imprisoned . . . or in any other way destroyed
   > . . . except by the lawful judgment of his peers or by the law of the land."
   >
   > —excerpt from Magna Carta

   Which constitutional principle is best expressed in this excerpt?
   A. trial by jury
   B. checks and balances
   C. popular sovereignty
   D. rule of law

2. What document was the first constitution of the United States?
   A. Magna Carta
   B. Mayflower Compact
   C. Declaration of Independence
   D. Articles of Confederation

3. What did the 13th, 14th, and 15th amendments have in common?
   A. All limited the power of the state governments.
   B. All aimed to protect the civil rights of former slaves.
   C. All increased the power of the states to end slavery.
   D. All intended to solve the problems created by Reconstruction.

4. What does a system of checks and balances do?
   A. divides governmental power among three different branches
   B. establishes a government based on the consent of the people
   C. creates national and state levels of governments
   D. gives each branch of government the power to limit other branches

5. What is the legal process by which a person can become a U.S. citizen?
   A. deportation
   B. adoption
   C. immigration
   D. naturalization

Document-Based Question

Read the document and answer the questions.

Citizenship in a democracy requires participation, civility, patience—rights as well as responsibilities. Political scientist Benjamin Barber has noted, "Democracy is often understood as the rule of the majority, and rights are understood more and more as the private possessions of individuals. . . . But this is to misunderstand both rights and democracy." For democracy to succeed, citizens must be active, not passive, because they know that the success or failure of the government is their responsibility, and no one else's.

It is certainly true that individuals exercise basic rights—such as freedom of speech, assembly, religion—but in another sense, rights, like individuals, do not function in isolation. Rights are exercised within the framework of a society, which is why rights and responsibilities are so closely connected.

Democratic government, which is elected by and accountable to its citizens, protects individual rights so that citizens in a democracy can undertake their civic obligations and responsibilities, thereby strengthening the society as a whole.

At a minimum, citizens should educate themselves about the critical issues confronting their society, if only so that they can vote intelligently. Some obligations, such as serving on juries in civil or criminal trials or in the military, may be required by law, but most are voluntary.

—U.S. Department of State, *USA Democracy in Brief*

6a. What does this document suggest might happen to individual rights if citizen's ignore their civic obligations and responsibilities?

_____

_____

_____

6b. What steps can a citizen take to be active, not passive?

_____

_____

_____

STOP

Multiple Choice

1. Use the table to answer the question.

Branch	Power
1.	Can veto proposed laws
2.	Can pass laws for the nation
3.	Can declare laws unconstitutional

Which of the following best completes the chart?

A. 1. Federal, 2. Confederal, 3. State

B. 1. Congress, 2. Senate, 3. House of Representatives

C. 1. Executive, 2. Legislative, 3. Judicial

D. 1. District Court, 2. Court of Appeals, 3. Supreme Court

2. Who holds the most powerful office in the House of Representatives?

A. Speaker of the House   **C.** President of the Senate

B. party whip   **D.** President Pro Tempore

3. Use the information in the box to answer the question.

How a Bill Becomes a Federal Law
1.   A conference merges the two bills.
2.   The House and Senate vote on the revised bill.
3.   The president, signs, vetoes or ignores the bill.
4.   Each house of Congress passes a version of a bill.

What is the correct sequence of events?

A. 3, 1, 4, 2   **C.** 2, 3, 4, 1

B. 4, 1, 2, 3   **D.** 1, 2, 4, 3

4. What role does the president perform as Commander in Chief?

A. heads the U.S. armed forces   **C.** appoints diplomats

B. proposes a national budget   **D.** grants pardons

5. Which Supreme Court decision established the power of judicial review and why is this power important?

A. *Brown* v. *Board of Education,* ended segregation in public schools

B. *Miranda* v. *Arizona,* stated that police must inform suspects of their rights

C. *Marbury* v. *Madison,* gave the court the power to declare a law unconstitutional

D. *Plessy* v. *Ferguson,* established that slaves could not sue in federal court

GO ON ▶

Document-Based Question

Read the document and answer the questions.

> All of us [Supreme Court Justices] appreciate that the institution we serve is far more important than the particular individuals who compose the Court's bench at any given time. And our job, in my view, is the best work a jurist anywhere could have. Our charge is to pursue justice as best we can. The Founding Fathers were wise enough to equip us to do that by according us life tenure (or, as the Constitution says, tenure "during good behavior") [a life-long appointment], and salaries that cannot be diminished while we hold office.
>
> Our former Chief Justice, William H. Rehnquist, spoke of the role of the judge using a sports metaphor:
>
> The Constitution has placed the judiciary in a position similar to that of a referee in a basketball game who is obliged to call a foul against a member of the home team at a critical moment in the game: he will be soundly booed, but he is nonetheless obliged to call it as he saw it, not as the home court crowd wants him to call it.
>
> The day any judge shirks from that responsibility, Chief Justice Rehnquist counseled, is the day he or she should resign from office. All members of today's Court would concur in that counsel.
>
> —Justice Ruth Bader Ginsburg, speech delivered on March 13, 2009

6a. What does Justice Ginsburg say is the main goal of the Supreme Court? Do you agree with the steps that the Founding Fathers took to protect these goals?

_____

_____

_____

6b. According to Justice Ginsburg, how is the role of the Supreme Court similar to a sports referee? Do you agree with this comparison? Explain.

_____

_____

_____

Multiple Choice

1. Use the quote to answer the question.

> The powers not delegated to the United States by the Constitution, nor prohibited by it to the States, are reserved to the States respectively, or to the people
>
> —U.S. Constitution, Amendment 10

What type of power does this quote describe?

A. delegated power   **C.** concurrent power

B. reserved power   **D.** implied powers

2. Which power is shared by both the state and national governments?

A. declaring war

B. collecting taxes

C. establishing local governments

D. issuing driver's licenses

3. Which is a duty of a state governor?

A. preside over the state senate

B. appoint heads to major political parties

C. distribute state funds to local schools

D. prepare a state's budget

4. Use the information in the box to answer the question.

> "Being fiscally responsible and keeping our city safe will always be two of my top priorities."

Which official would **most** likely make this statement?

A. governor   **C.** state senator

B. mayor   **D.** county commissioner

5. Which level of government is **most** responsible for providing police protection, fire departments, and trash collection?

A. federal   **C.** state

B. national   **D.** local

Document-Based Question

The diagram below shows the division of power in the division of powers in the American federal system. Examine the diagram and answer the questions.

National
- Declare war
- Maintain armed forces
- Regulate interstate and foreign trade
- Admit new states
- Establish post offices
- Set standard weights and measures
- Coin money
- Establish foreign policy
- Make all laws necessary and proper for carrying out delegated powers

Shared
- Maintain law and order
- Levy taxes
- Borrow money
- Charter banks
- Establish courts
- Provide for public welfare

State
- Establish and maintain schools
- Establish local governments
- Regulate business within the state
- Make marriage laws
- Provide for public safety
- Assume other powers not delegated to the national government nor prohibited to the states

6a. How do the powers of the national government differ from those reserved for the states?

_____

_____

_____

6b. Why do you think both levels of government share some powers, such as the power to levy taxes?

_____

_____

_____

Multiple Choice

1. Use the quote to answer the question.

> "[Party loyalty] serves always to distract the public councils and enfeeble the public administration. It agitates the Community with ill-founded jealousies and false alarms . . ."
> —President George Washington's Farewell Address, 1796

Which statement best summarizes Washington's views of political parties?

A. A two-party system is essential to democracy.

B. Parties must compromise to work together.

C. Wealthy citizens use political parties to serve their interests.

D. Parties can divide people and weaken government.

2. Which of the following is a role of a political party?

A. nominate political candidates

B. form agreements with other parties

C. finance government services

D. limit campaign contributions

3. What is the most important way that American citizens can participate in government?

A. volunteering

B. working for an interest group

C. voting in elections

D. running for office

4. What is the largest source of revenue for the national government?

A. social security taxes

B. income taxes

C. property taxes

D. estate taxes

5. What results when government spends more money than it collects?

A. a surplus

B. a balanced budget

C. a deficit

D. an audit

GO ON

Document-Based Question

Examine the cartoon and answer the questions.

© Jeff Parker/Florida Today

6a. How does the cartoonist illustrate public opinion and its effect on the Brevard County Commission?

_____

_____

_____

6b. According to this cartoon, do you think the citizens of Brevard County supported the beach parking fee?

_____

_____

_____

_____

Multiple Choice

1. Which tool is used by families and nations to decide the best way to spend money?
   A. a budget
   B. a scheduled payment
   C. an allowance Allowances
   D. an appropriation

2. Which level of government is responsible for making laws that regulate marriage and divorce?
   A. federal
   B. state
   C. local
   D. city

3. Which U.S. Supreme Court decision established that juveniles have the same rights as adults?
   A. *Brown* v. *Board of Education*
   B. *In re Gault*
   C. *Miranda* v. *Arizona*
   D. *Gideon* v. *Wainwright*

4. What must a police officer have before arresting a suspect?
   A. probable cause
   B. an indictment
   C. an arraignment
   D. a plea bargain

5. Use the table to answer the question.

Homicide Arrests by Age

Age Group	2005	2009
Under 18 years of age	844	803
18 years of age and over	8,340	7,537
Total all ages	9,184	8,340

Source: FBI: *Crime in the United States*

How many juvenile offenders were arrested for homicide in 2009?
   A. 803
   B. 844
   C. 7,537
   D. 8,340

GO ON

Document-Based Question

The volunteers in the photo below are providing assistance to residents of Volusia County, Florida, whose homes were damaged by a hurricane Examine the photograph and answer the questions.

© Jeff Parker/Florida Today

6a. How does this photograph show citizens participating in their community?

_____

_____

_____

6b. Why do you think many Americans feel that volunteering in their communities is an important part of citizenship?

_____

_____

_____

Multiple Choice

1. Which principle states that businesses provide more products when they can sell them at higher prices?

    A. law of supply

    B. law of demand

    C. law of competition

    D. law of scarcity

2. Which of the following is true of the free-enterprise system?

    A. The government tells businesses what to produce.

    B. People are able to run their business in the way they think best

    C. It has led to economic success in North Korea and Cuba.

    D. Businesses face little competition.

3. Which common feature characterizes a nation's currency?

    A. being in short supply

    B. considered legal tender

    C. can be used in all nations

    D. has different values across regions

4. What system did Congress establish to regulate the U.S. banking system?

    A. Social Security System

    B. Circular Flow System

    C. Social Insurance System

    D. Federal Reserve System

5. Which term is used to refer to the government's policy for collecting and spending money?

    A. monetary policy

    B. banking policy

    C. fiscal policy

    D. the business cycle

Document-Based Question

Read the document and answer the questions.

> At stake is whether new jobs and industries take root in this country, or somewhere else. It's whether the hard work and industry of our people is rewarded. It's whether we sustain the leadership that has made America not just a place on a map, but the light to the world.
>
> We are poised for progress. Two years after the worst recession most of us have ever known, the stock market has come roaring back. Corporate profits are up. The economy is growing again.
>
> But we have never measured progress by these yardsticks alone. We measure progress by the success of our people. By the jobs they can find and the quality of life those jobs offer. By the prospects of a small business owner who dreams of turning a good idea into a thriving enterprise. By the opportunities for a better life that we pass on to our children. . . .
>
> Thanks to the tax cuts we passed, Americans' paychecks are a little bigger today. Every business can write off the full cost of new investments that they make this year. And these steps, taken by Democrats and Republicans, will grow the economy and add to the more than one million private sector jobs created last year. . . .
>
> The competition for jobs is real. But this shouldn't discourage us. It should challenge us. Remember—for all the hits we've taken these last few years, for all the naysayers predicting our decline, America still has the largest, most prosperous economy in the world. No workers—no workers are more productive than ours. No country has more successful companies, or grants more patents to inventors and entrepreneurs. We're the home to the world's best colleges and universities, where more students come to study than any place on Earth.
>
> —President Barack Obama, State of the Union address, January 25, 2011

6a. How does Obama say Americans should measure the country's economic strength?

_____

_____

6b. The U.S. economy goes through business cycles of expansion and contraction. According to this speech, what was the status of the U.S. economy in this cycle in January, 2011?

_____

_____

Multiple Choice

1. Use the information in the box to answer the question.

> Title:_____
> - Promote World Peace
> - Maintain National Security
> - Support Democracy
> - Provide Aid

Which title best completes this list?

A. The President's Foreign Policy Powers

B. Congressional Foreign Policy Powers

C. Four Goals of Foreign Policy

D. Main Types of Foreign Alliances

2. Which of the following is a diplomatic tool of foreign policy?

A. taking military action

B. withholding money

C. banning trade

D. maintaining embassies

3. Which foreign policy power can be executed by Congress?

A. approve funding for foreign aid

B. make peace treaties

C. establish executive agreements

D. declare war

4. What international organization was founded after World War II to promote worldwide peace and cooperation?

A. The League of Nations

B. The United Nations

C. The International Court of Justice

D. North Atlantic Treaty Association.

5. What threat was the policy of containment designed to stop?

A. détente

C. Vietnam War

B. nuclear war

D. communism

GO ON

Document-Based Question

Read the document and answer the questions.

> Immediately following the first attack, I implemented our government's emergency response plans. Our military is powerful, and it's prepared. Our emergency teams are working in New York City and Washington, D.C., to help with local rescue efforts.
>
> Our first priority is to get help to those who have been injured and to take every precaution to protect our citizens at home and around the world from further attacks.
>
> The functions of our government continue without interruption. Federal agencies in Washington, which had to be evacuated today, are reopening for essential personnel tonight and will be open for business tomorrow.
>
> Our financial institutions remain strong, and the American economy will be open for business as well.
>
> The search is under way for those who are behind these evil acts. I've directed the full resources for our intelligence and law enforcement communities to find those responsible and bring them to justice. We will make no distinction between the terrorists who committed these acts and those who harbor them.
>
> —President George W. Bush, addressing the country after terrorist attacks, September 11, 2001

6a. What groups does President Bush identify as part of the government's emergency response plans? Which groups will likely act internationally?

_____

_____

_____

6b. Less than a month after this address, President Bush announced a global war on terror to be led by the United States and its allies. How does that announcement relate to the message included in this address?

_____

_____

_____

STOP